Smart Cities

Martin Gitlin

CHERRY LAKE PRESS

Published in the United States of America by Cherry Lake Publishing
Ann Arbor, Michigan
www.cherrylakepublishing.com

Reading Adviser: Marla Conn, MS, Ed., Literacy specialist, Read-Ability, Inc.

Photo Credits: © jamesteohart/Shutterstock, cover, 1; © Singapore Buses/Flickr, 6; © Massimo Catarinela/WikiMedia, 7; © Fred J Productions/Shutterstock, 10; © franz12/Shutterstock, 12; © Andrey Bayda/Shutterstock, 15; © David Prado Perucha/Shutterstock, 17; © Tavarius/Shutterstock, 18; © traxlergirl/Shutterstock, 21; © Golden Brown/Shutterstock, 23; © Konstantin Tronin/Shutterstock, 24; © Matthew Talboys/Shutterstock, 27; © Jorge Salcedo/Shutterstock, 29

Graphic Element Credits: © Ohn Mar/Shutterstock.com, back cover, multiple interior pages;
© Dmitrieva Katerina/Shutterstock.com, back cover, multiple interior pages;
© advent/Shutterstock.com, back cover, front cover, multiple interior pages;
© Visual Generation/Shutterstock.com, multiple interior pages;
© anfisa focusova/Shutterstock.com, front cover, multiple interior pages;
© Babich Alexander/Shutterstock.com, back cover, front cover, multiple interior pages

Library of Congress Cataloging-in-Publication Data

Names: Gitlin, Marty, author.
Title: Smart cities / by Martin Gitlin.
Description: Ann Arbor, Michigan : Cherry Lake Publishing, [2020] | Series:
  Exploring the Internet of Things | Includes bibliographical references
  and index. | Audience: Grades 4-6.
Identifiers: LCCN 2020003055 (print) | LCCN 2020003056 (ebook) | ISBN
  9781534168954 (hardcover) | ISBN 9781534170636 (paperback) | ISBN
  9781534172470 (pdf) | ISBN 9781534174313 (ebook)
Subjects: LCSH: Smart cities—Juvenile literature.
Classification: LCC TD159.4 .G58 2020 (print) | LCC TD159.4 (ebook) | DDC
  307.760285—dc23
LC record available at https://lccn.loc.gov/2020003055
LC ebook record available at https://lccn.loc.gov/2020003056

Printed in the United States of America
Corporate Graphics

Table of Contents

Introduction

People are attracted to big cities. They're full of vibrant life. Big cities have science and art museums. They host parades. But all this comes at a cost. Big cities around the world struggle to provide services for the millions of people they attract.

More than half the people in the world live in cities. And the numbers keep growing. About two-thirds of the global population are projected to be city dwellers by 2050. The result would be 2.5 billion more city residents. That means even greater challenges to coordinating everyone's needs.

One of the biggest problems facing our cities is keeping them clean. Garbage collection from homes is costly and time-consuming. Trash often litters the streets. According to *The World Bank*, our global waste will increase to 3.7 billion tons by 2050. That's equivalent to more than 1 billion African elephants! Factories still spew pollution into the air and water. A difficult job awaits cities that seek to handle such

Most cities battle stop-and-go traffic due to high population.

problems as millions more people arrive. We also have trouble coordinating when trash collectors come, how often, and at what cost.

Another issue is traffic. City roads and highways have been trying to solve this problem for decades. Cars and trucks are often at a standstill. The **influx** of people into urban centers threatens to worsen driver frustration. An Urban Mobility Report from the Texas A&M Transportation Institute shows that the average driver in Los Angeles, California, will spend 119 hours each year stuck in traffic!

Cities face many other questions. One revolves around basic energy. City planners and leaders must decide the best energy sources for their communities. The options are growing. Among

According to research, the top smart cities and countries include London, England; Singapore; and Barcelona, Spain. Pictured is one of Singapore's autonomous buses.

them are wind, **solar**, and nuclear power. Clean energy such as wind and solar have been embraced in many cities. But there are still huge challenges ahead if we want to reduce the 900 million tons of coal that U.S. electricity plants use every year.

The Internet of Things (IoT) is one way we can overcome these challenges. IoT has begun to transform struggling cities into smart cities. Many cities around the world have used IoT **technology** to make positive changes. IoT has the potential to alter every aspect of city life.

Smart cities provide innovative solutions. In Amsterdam, Netherlands, the street lamps dim based on usage.

CHAPTER ONE

IoT in and Around the City

European cities took the lead in creatively using IoT technology. These cities have connected objects and machines that transmit **data** using wireless technology and the **cloud**.

What's the purpose of connecting objects to the internet? One goal is to help the environment. Another is to make lives simpler and better. Citizens work together by using smartphones and mobile devices to gather data for the city. For example, traffic flow is improved when **GPS** systems can tell how many people are on certain roads based on the number of smartphone signals it finds there. Citizens use connected cars and homes to make decisions that help themselves and their communities. Rideshare **apps**, like Uber and Lyft, reduce individual **emissions** and help keep our air clean. Across the globe, cities that use public transportation have become even cleaner. With real-time

In order for a city to become "smart," the local government would need to invest a lot of money in IoT technology *and* infrastructure.

Using public transportation means less cars on the road, less traffic, and less polluted air.

schedules and bus apps, people have an easier time traveling in cities. All this and more have been made possible through IoT technology.

Copenhagen, Denmark, is a shining example of IoT in action. The Denmark capital has launched many smart projects. For instance, the city's use of smart traffic signals promotes biking and public transportation. IoT-connected traffic signals have **sensors** that allow bikers and buses to pass through faster than cars. They receive data from sensors that show traffic patterns in real time. That helps traffic move at a much faster pace. People might think twice about driving to work, especially if they're running late!

Parking meters can also be embedded with sensors. Drivers learn from their connected cars where there is an open parking spot.

Beyond automobiles, bike riding also cuts down on gas emissions. Sensors embedded in the streets of Copenhagen can help **monitor** air quality and tell residents when there has been a decrease in greenhouse gas emissions. It lets people know they are helping to create a cleaner and more efficient community. The University of California, Davis, has found that if more people biked to work, we could reduce greenhouse gas emissions 11 percent by 2050.

In the Netherlands, the city of Amsterdam is also focusing on **sustainability** through the use of IoT technology. Its floating village of houses solved the problem of overcrowding. A floating village is a man-made island. It is anchored by concrete tubs that go down about 20 feet (6 meters) into the water, with a steel foundation on top to build lightweight homes. Expanding out into the ocean ensures that there is room for everyone. Shared IoT data in these villages allows its residents to be more energy efficient.

Helping the environment could be the most important benefit of smart technology. But its abilities extend into other areas as well. In social spaces, IoT technology has made life

There are even smart garbage cans that help cities lessen traffic and trash buildup.

easier for people to connect with one another and navigate the city they call home. That is important because the fast-paced world of city life can be difficult on your own.

Even garbage cans have joined the IoT world! They send data to waste management companies when they are full. Only then do they schedule pickup from garbage collectors. That saves time and energy. It also means less transportation for the trash collectors, which reduces gas emissions from their trucks that pollute the air.

Amsterdam and Copenhagen are not the only big European cities to have embraced IoT technology. Other smart cities include London, England; Paris, France; and Berlin, Germany. These cities proved more **progressive** in IoT technology than the world. However, not all cities have the funds or resources to **implement** IoT technology. Certain organizations have created monetary prizes so cities can receive the funds they need to become IoT capable.

American cities like New York, New York, have joined the ranks too. It's the largest city in the United States. The city and its people have been eager to use IoT to deal with massive traffic issues. New York has planned to place cameras all over the city to monitor traffic in real time. The connected devices promise to help vehicles, including buses, pass through the city's streets quickly and easily. Sensors will also let equipment managers know when devices are about to break down by sending out a signal that they need maintenance. That means less work for road crews and fewer lane closures for sensor repairs.

Perhaps one day, cities of all sizes will be smart cities. The process is expensive. The technology has not been perfected. But IoT cities are not just the future; many have already arrived.

WHEN LIFE GETS TOO LOUD

There is another type of pollution aside from what's in the air and water: noise pollution. Many people are bothered by the loud noise in city spaces. For example, music or fireworks coming from outdoor stadiums bother people who are trying to work or sleep.

Smart technology can help. Sensors placed near bars where loud music plays or near where construction sites operate can monitor noise levels. They can also be used near sports or rock concert venues. This allows people with noise sensitivities to avoid loud areas.

Beyond IoT, the problem with monitoring noise levels is finding a solution. One would be to create policies that limit the loudness of band music in nightclubs and at outdoor concerts.

New York is known as "the city that never sleeps."

CHAPTER TWO

Benefits and Drawbacks

Smart cities make life easier and better for its residents. In addition to creating cleaner air and water, and helping traffic, IoT technology can improve emergency services. Think about a woman who is about to have a baby. It's important that she reach the hospital quickly. When traffic lights are connected and timed to keep cars moving, she can be sure to reach her destination faster.

Even simple streetlights could be transformed into smart devices. Wireless IoT connections can extend streetlight use beyond simply lighting streets. Smart streetlights could send data that alerts drivers about traffic problems ahead. They could provide severe weather warnings. Smart streetlights could also detect open parking spaces. In San Diego, California, smart streetlights are being used for this very reason, and can even tell when someone is parked illegally. All of this information could be sent directly to devices like smartphones.

Smart traffic lights can communicate with each other and readjust after power failures.

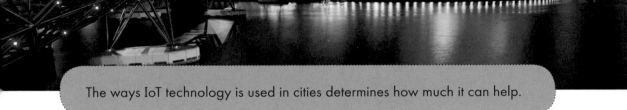

The ways IoT technology is used in cities determines how much it can help.

Smart technology brings people together. They share wide-ranging data. They communicate from connected cars and homes. The result is citizens and technology coming together to create tighter-knit communities. People *and* technology can work together to make life better on our planet.

IoT technology can also create safer communities. This has been proven in California. Firefighters used **drones** to take aerial shots of wildfires near San Francisco. This allowed them to battle the blaze more efficiently by pinpointing where it was strongest. Another example is when data from sensors informed Los Angeles traffic planners about dangerous intersections for bikers and **pedestrians**. The result was added officers and bike lanes in those areas.

IoT technology can even help the police department keep cities safer. In Boston, Massachusetts, sensors in a gunfire detection system are placed around the city in various locations. This system alerts police officers of crime scenes within seconds.

Smart data also has connected city officials, businesses, and residents through public safety monitoring systems. IoT can protect people and provide emergency support. That does not mean there are no drawbacks. Cities become vulnerable to hacks or cyberattacks. People who want to keep their information private may fear security breaches.

Another concern revolves around the accuracy of the data itself. Smart cities hope that information received from IoT sources is accurate. Only then can it turn into positive action. City officials must make good decisions based on that data. Smart cities need smart humans to make them work.

Those involved with implementing and running smart cities will make mistakes. Experience is the best teacher. The result should be that they make more of a positive impact as time goes on.

A SMART CITY WINNER

New York is not the only huge American city to launch IoT projects. Others include Los Angeles and San Francisco, California; Chicago, Illinois; and Boston, Massachusetts. But more cities have started incorporating the new technology.

One of them is Columbus, Ohio. That city won the 2016 U.S. Department of Transportation Smart City Challenge. The result was millions of dollars in funding for 2020. Columbus intends to launch projects that will transform its transportation system. The city has purchased a fleet of electric smart cars that are **eco-friendly**. The idea is to use IoT technology to help traffic run smoothly through the city. A study done by the National Science Foundation found that cars with self-driving features greatly reduced traffic jams. The smart cars flowed at a constant speed while the non-smart cars had more stop-and-go traffic.

Columbus received a lot of money to improve the lives of its residents, grow its economy, and provide better access to job opportunities using IoT technology.

CHAPTER THREE

The Future of Smart Cities

By 2015, several cities in Europe had been using IoT technology for many years. The U.S. Department of Transportation decided that American cities needed to join the ranks. So, it created the Smart City Challenge. The government office would award $40 million to the city with the best IoT plan for its transportation system. A total of 78 cities applied. They listed their biggest challenges to show their need for funds. The 2016 winner was Columbus, Ohio. They are using their winnings to improve transportation services, to make them safer, more efficient, and accessible to all.

Another competition soon began. The Smart City Council created its own contest that benefitted many cities. The council offered workshops. It also provided online tools to help plan, manage, and finance IoT projects.

Such challenges spurred many American cities to research the new technology. Their ideas extended far beyond

Turning a city into a "smart city" is a huge project, and lots of different city departments have to be on board.

IoT can help plan and combat disasters like wildfires.

transportation needs. They proved that IoT technology was the future for cities across the country.

One example of effective IoT usage is Miami, Florida. Rising sea levels there have motivated action. They are rising by 1 to 3 inches (2.5 to 7.6 centimeters) every 3 years. That might not seem like a lot, but it can have devastating consequences for wildlife and communities. The city has installed waterfront sensors and other data sources to identify vulnerable areas. Officials can now defend itself from tidal flooding.

Earthquakes are a major problem in California. Sensors have been placed throughout the state to predict when earthquakes will strike and how far the damage will travel. That information can be crucial to emergency response systems. Major quakes can jam the doors of fire stations and delay response times. But IoT alert devices give warning. They can connect to fire station doors and allow them to open in the event of a quake.

Each smart city must decide how IoT technology can solve their specific problems. The success of smart cities will ultimately depend on making smart decisions about smart technology.

Canada launched its own Smart City Challenge in 2019. Montreal won, and was awarded $50 million for its proposal to improve public transportation and access to food.

Nunavut, Canada, was also a Smart City Challenge winner. The suicide rate in Nunavut is 10 times greater than the national average. The goal of their IoT proposal was to prevent suicides. Ultimately, they were awarded $10 million for a project that teaches a love for living.

Nunavut's proposal would use connected devices to provide better access to mental health resources. This includes peer networks, mobile apps, and even digital art therapy. Each outlet would help those who are struggling with their mental health. This is an example of using IoT to let others know that they are not alone.

GOING UP OR DOWN?

One IoT device that will bring peace of mind is the smart elevator. The need for more efficient elevators in New York City has been obvious for some time. Traditional elevators force people to press a button and wait for it to arrive. Then they crowd together, sometimes stopping on every floor to let out or add more people.

In smart elevators, people could pick the floor they wish to reach, and the system would let them know which elevator would get them there faster. Smart elevators also promise to sense when the elevator is getting crowded. It would then skip floors so more people could not get on after it is full. That would save time for people who are already on the elevator.

Some of this technology is already in use. Smart elevator companies have been working on these issues and are already making money doing it. Research shows that in 2020, they will earn about $23 billion. The technology is still young, though, and is expected to really take off by 2025.

The Crystal, a smart building in London, England, is so sustainable that its heating bill is zero dollars.

Creativity and Innovation

Cities seeking benefits from IoT technology must decide how their money should be spent. Their needs depend on many factors. They could be affected by weather in their region or by specific problems that face the communities.

City officials will be asking many questions in the future. They will be hiring experts in IoT technology who will be looking for answers. Decisions made will positively or negatively impact their cities for decades.

Think About It

What IoT device would you invent that would benefit the community you live in?

Smart cities would help the environment, increase safety, streamline transportation, and provide more efficient use of energy.

Learn More

Books

Gleeson, Bridget, Nicola Williams, et al. *The Cities Book: A Journey Through 86 of the World's Greatest Cities*. London: Lonely Planet Kids, 2016.

Menzies, Lucy. *Cities Around the World: A Global Search and Find Book*. London, England: Ivy Kids, 2019.

Tardif, Benoit. *Metropolis*. Tonawanda, NY: Kids Can Press, 2016.

Websites

Internet of Things Facts for Kids
https://kids.kiddle.co/Internet_of_things
Discover more facts about IoT technology.

What Is a Smart City?
https://mocomi.com/what-is-a-smart-city
Learn more about smart cities and what it means.

Glossary

apps (APS) computer applications for mobile systems and devices

cloud (KLOUD) data that is stored on the internet

data (DAY-tuh) facts to be used for planning or making decisions

drones (DROHNZ) unmanned controlled aircraft used for a variety of purposes

eco-friendly (EE-koh-frend-lee) good for the environment

emissions (ih-MISH-uhnz) pollutants spewed from cars and factories into the air

implement (IM-pluh-ment) to put a plan into action

influx (IN-fluks) the arrival or inward flow of a large amount of something

monitor (MAH-nih-tur) to check on or keep track of something

pedestrians (puh-DES-tree-uhnz) people who travel on foot

progressive (pruh-GRES-iv) desire to show progress or move forward

sensors (SEN-surz) detection devices that respond by transmitting a signal

solar (SOH-lur) related to the sun

sustainability (suh-stay-nuh-BIL-ih-tee) keeping something going for long periods of time

technology (tek-NAH-luh-jee) related to applying knowledge about science and industry

Index